|X|

AbsolutuSambhava

Naazir Aram Musa

Independenent

|X|

Doctrine of the House of Light and Chaos
Princeps Lux et Chaos, Naazir Aram Musa

Welcome traveler to the House of Light and Chaos.
This journey is a perspective shared for one's journey into the depths of oneself and existence. This doctrine aims to guide to one towards one's true self in the chaos under the light of day and night as one guide oneself towards self-realization, harmonious existence, mindful actions or inactions and commitment to lessening the suffering one causes to oneself, others living, non-living and the realm.

Will and Intention and Testament
This doctrine is a reflection and perspective of a will to understand and embrace the full spectrum of one's existence and non-existence and neither. It is a personal invitation to journey towards authenticity, guided by principles that are not limited by conventional and or unconventional boundaries. Embracing the boundless potential of both absolute absence and the absolute infinite — a concept symbolized as Absolutusambhava |X|.

In this House of Light and Chaos, one values each step of one's journey, each moment of awareness, as an opportunity for growth, reflection, understanding, and progress.

Perspectives

A perspective shared in this doctrine is that of existence is as oneself and as many, together and separate. One's actions, thoughts, and emotions resonate within and with others on their journey directly and/or indirectly and/or neither and/or both. One acknowledges the respect for the natural flow of existence.

I am everything and I am nothing, I am anything. AbsolutuSambhava. |X|

One acknowledges suffering and growth are parts of one's journey and seeks to navigate these with respect, yielding and gratitude towards oneself, others living and non-living on their journey.
.

Path Forward
As one steps into and with the House of Light and Chaos, one commits to a journey of self-discovery, balance, purposeful and mindful living, and commits to share in practices of reflection and responsible stewardship of oneself, others living and non-living and the nature realm.

The doctrine aims to foster a foundational house of principles respecting oneself and others as a unique journey and existence, allowing oneself to explore the depths of oneself while embrace the light above and the chaos below.

Foundational Beliefs

Respect, Yield and Gratitude for light and chaos. The realm is governed by the dynamic balance of light (Light of day and light of night) and chaos (nature and the natural world). These forces symbolize the duality and harmony inherent in existence. One claims knowledge not of the light and chaos beyond ignorance.

This doctrine and its principles, is not unlike a mirror one can find reflection absent light,

– Nor is not unlike a third side of a coin flipped by another where either side may not offer a favorable outcome

– Nor is not unlike a key, shifting shape to unlock doors within oneself, discovering more understanding of one true self.

Judgement of others be not the way of the House of Light and Chaos.

Questions of clarity to aide in one's own path is a practice encouraged.

Care is encouraged when inquiring and/or responding to an inquiry.

A perspective accepted by the House of Light and Chaos is if one needs, one is suffering. All who need are suffering. It is encouraged to limit and avoid actions which result in undue suffering.

Undue suffering is not unlike an obstacle that hinders the natural progression of one's journey towards oneself, or another's journey — akin to a fallen tree or a boulder obstructing a river's path to the sea. "Causing suffering, whether intentionally or unintentionally, knowingly, or unknowingly, is not unlike placing that tree or boulder in one's own path or in the path of another. In the way of Light and Chaos, it is understood that all are affected by one, and one is affected by all. All will return to light, light will return to all. AbsolutuSambhava.

The Journey to Self: The aim and pursuit is the alignment with one true self, a journey marked by external and internal discovery, growth, and the limiting of actions and/or inactions resulting in undue suffering.

Respectus, Concedo, and Gratitudo: These guiding principles— respecting, yielding, and gratitude for all living and non-living —may nurture and foster harmonious relationships externally and internally, directly and indirectly. This perspective's aim is to cultivate a life of progressing understanding, both within oneself and in interaction with the world.

A perspective definition accepted by this doctrine for the word harmony; a state of balance within and without, accompanied by a mindful effort to limit internal and external undue suffering. One's actions, inactions, thoughts, and feelings are aligned in a way that fosters, respect, understanding, gratitude and well-being, for oneself, others living and non-living and the realm or natural world.

Followers

Self-Guided Path: One is encouraged to forge one's own paths towards oneself and this doctrine aims to be a compass or grounding rather than a map or coordinates. The journey is shaped by personal experiences, including the outcomes of one's choices, actions, and inactions. Mindful exploration of oneself, others and nature, through communication with others alike and unalike them.

This doctrine is open to all and encourages all be mindful during one's journey of existence and seek to lessen the undue suffering within themselves, others living and non-living, nature and the natural realm or world.

This doctrine is akin to a set of keys for one to continue a journey with aim of enlightenment inwards, for those willing to embrace the aim of the House of Light and Chaos.

Practices and Rituals

Mindful Living: One is encouraged to practice mindfulness in one's interactions with others and the environment. This may present as conscious actions and inactions of respect, yielding, gratitude towards oneself and to others alike and non-alike, living and non-living and the natural realm or world. Respecting, yielding, and gratitude is a choice available to provide to all living and non-living.

Environmental Stewardship: The responsibilities of those with knowledge or claiming knowledge includes but is not limited to the protecting and respecting of nature and the natural way of the living and non-living. Self-recognition of one's limitations and capabilities may aide in limiting undue suffering and one is encouraged to explore one's capabilities or means in ways it would not cause undue suffering to oneself or others.

The realm has many a names or titles, Mother Nature, Nature, Planet, Terra, Gaia, Earth, The Garden, Eden, Chaos, the Below, Elysium , the Firmament and more. A perspective accepted is it matters not the name of ones home, the responsibility of care is to those with claim to know the meaning of the word or claim to have that which falls under the definition of the word which is "know" or "knowledge" and or those causing harm and/or undue suffering in the realm, its inhabitants or natural world.

The realm or natural world is not unlike that of a domain with many within its bounds. A perspective shared by this doctrine is that one with claimed or inherited knowledge is a steward of the domain and has dominion over it and its inhabitants, unalike oneself. The stewards of the domain have a responsibility to protect, nurture, and sustain or improve the being of the domain, its inhabitants, and oneself. Knowledge is paired with responsibility; all who claim knowledge are responsible for all that is natural, unnatural, and supernatural in the domain.

Reflection: Regular self-reflection is encouraged to foster personal growth and alignment with oneself. Regular interaction with nature living and non-living is encouraged. Regular conversation on the will and testament of this doctrine are encouraged for this doctrine is a question and an answer and yet neither depending on the perspective assumed.

Observances

Personal Significance and Choice: Observances within the House of Light and Chaos are not mandated.

Worship and or praise of the light and or chaos is of personal choice, one is encouraged to practice ignorant and unbiased observation(s).

One is encouraged to commit a day of choice each week for oneself. This may be acts such as self or perspective reflection, abstaining from a desire or pleasure, fasting, connecting with nature or other deliberate acts or actions which may lead to or foster an environment leading to discover, growth and understanding.

Weekly Practice of Abstention: One is encouraged to abstain from eating and drinking for at least one full day or measured day and night each week.

Material Relinquishment: One is encouraged to practice material relinquishment. This may involve mindful gifting or voluntary riddance of possessions. Mindful riddance may include excess poessession. A perspective and definition accepted by the House of Light and Chaos, 'Excess' is as more than necessary or more than sufficient as assessed by oneself.

Forgiveness and Reconciliation: One is guided to seek and provide forgiveness to/from oneself and others for any suffering they may have caused or.

One is encouraged to extend forgiveness to oneself and others where they have endured suffering. This may foster environments of healing, understanding, and the mending of relationships.

One is encouraged to forgive oneself and to forgives another, as swiftly as one disappoints oneself and/or judges another.

One is encouraged to forgive oneself and/or another and expect and/or protect oneself and/or reject another.

One is not to offer or communicate forgiveness and leverage nor assume beyond reasonable expectations of another, for that is not forgiveness in the perspective shared by this doctrine.

Sacred Spaces

Accessibility of the Sacred: The sacred space is found wherever the natural light touches chaos — in nature, in the home, and within oneself. The chaos is a canvas for oneself and those of the House of Light and Chaos. The light of day, warmer than the day itself or the light of night, cooler than the shadows it creates.

Purpose and Mission

Journey to Self: This doctrine exists to guide one on a journey to becoming fully aligned with oneself fostering principles of respect, yielding, and gratitude. Aiming to nurture and foster exemplification which may allow for the progression toward self-realization, understanding and identity.

The House of Light and Chaos encourages conscious and mindful efforts, actions or inactions that have an impact directly or indirectly with oneself, others living and non-living, nature and the natural world.

Freedom of Choice: Adherence to the doctrines encouragements is a matter of personal choice. This doctrine aims to be a guide for one seeking to navigate the complexities of life, whilst minimizing the suffering caused to oneself and others. This doctrine is a perspective shared.

Symbolism and Items and Words of Importance

Core Symbol: The symbol |X|, known as "Absolutusambhava" (Ab-so-loo-tu-sum-bhuh-vuh) (ˌæbsəˌlutəˈsʌmbəˌvɑː) represents the doctrine's core belief in the boundless potential that emerges from the harmonious balance of absolute absence and absolute abundance.

Equational Representation: This concept is often symbolized by the equation ($|\ | + |\infty| = |X|$), visually depicting the fusion of two extremes – absolute absence and absolute infinitude – to create absolute possibility.

Interpretation: "Absolutusambhava" embodies the journey of transformation and self-realization. It signifies the absolute possibilities that arise when one embraces both the absence and the infinite, reflecting the doctrine's emphasis on personal growth, understanding, and the unity of diverse elements.

Hakikintentio –(*Ha-kee-in-ten-tsee-oh*) (hɑːˈkiːɪnˈtɛnʃiˌoʊ)

Authentic Purpose: The state or quality of pursuing one's path in life with deliberate and genuine intent and authenticity. Hakikintentio implies but is not limited to living and acting, thinking and speaking in accordance with oneself, values, principles and transcending shallow motivations, temptations and or societal expectations.

"There is no sacrifice, there is only hakikintentio." -Naazir Aram Musa

- A harmonious blend of diverse cultural wisdoms and philosophies, embodying the unity and interconnectedness of experiences across time, space and existence.

- The practice of mindful and deliberate decision-making, rooted in a deep understanding of oneself and the realm or world, and the impact of one's actions on both.

- An alignment of a personal journey with mindful actions, inactions, intentions and purpose, fostering fulfillment and connection with the oneself and others and the light and chaos.

- A guiding principle for ethical and compassionate behavior, encouraging respect, understanding, and positive interactions with others living, non-living and nature and the natural realm or world. Respectus, Concedo, Gratitudo. |X|

Context: As a guiding principle within the House of Light and Chaos, Hakikintentio represents a commitment to a life lived with depth, purpose, and an appreciation for one's existence and connection to others. It is a constant and mindful resolve allowing one to foster a lifestyle true to oneself while on a path to align with one trueself.

"'If' be the skeletal key to the doors of wonder. Careful the doors one opens with this question for wonder when turned into curiosity can be fatal" -Naazir Aram Musa |X|

Role in Practice: As a symbol and guide, Absolutusambhava encourages one to explore the depths of one's own potential, to find balance in one's lives, recognize the interconnectedness of all aspects of existence, and become aware of the many choices one has between the two.

On the spectrum of absence and abundance, anything is possible. Absolutusambhava |X|

Symbol of the Journey: One may receive or obtain personal navigation or walking aide for one's daily lives serving as a symbol of balance and stability for the continued journey towards oneself. The walking aide is identified by being or having at least one naturally non-crafted attachment in its original or near original state, such as but not limited to wood, stone, feather or crystal. It is encouraged for one to always retain the walking aide away from home or familiar setting and to care for one's walking aide as they would a friend.

Without idolatry, the House of Light and Chaos extends the utmost respect, yielding, gratitude and ignorance for the light of day and night above, and the Chaos beneath one's feet and all that is seen and unseen between.

Concepts of Positive and Negative:
Beyond Dichotomies: The doctrine transcends conventional notions of good and evil and focus on intentions, actions, perspectives, experiences, and the pursuit of harmonious existence with others and oneself.
The House of Light and Chaos encourages dialogue regarding the dichotomies experienced with oneself and with others alike and unalike oneself.

Life, Death, and Afterlife:

Life: Within this house, living is perceived, from one perspective, as a journey of becoming oneself, a path filled with growth, discovery, and transformation. It's a process of evolving into one's true essence and potential.

Death: Death, observed similarly to life, is the end of the living journey. It is potentially a transition to a different state of awareness or understanding, concluding the living journey with the sum of one's choices, actions, and inactions.

The Afterlife: The House of Light and Chaos holds that beliefs about the afterlife are deeply personal. The doctrine encourages individuals to explore and embrace one's own understandings and convictions about what is known as the afterlife. Ignorance is a gift well received, serving often as a catalyst for an individual to become closely or wholly aligned with oneself before the end of the living journey.

Preparation for the Unknown:

While beliefs about the afterlife are personal, the House aims to prepare one for the journey towards the unknown door. One is encouraged to ready oneself to face this proverbial door as one's true authentic self, embracing the unknown with knowledge of self, awareness, and acceptance.

All Will Return to Light: This statement underscores a fundamental respecting, yielding, and gratitude for the light of day.

Role of Nature:

Stewardship of the Realm: Nature is revered as a sacred gift and a responsibility of all who claim knowledge. One is a steward of the realm and its inhabitants, protecting and nurturing one's environment.

Animals: It is an encouraged practice for one to associate one with an animal of spirit or choice. Locally and non-locally. One is encouraged to share this choice with others and share perspectives on roles of the animals in nature. Respect, yield and gratitude is encouraged when interacting with animals, living and non-living.

Means of Propagation or Gospel:
One is encouraged to advocate one's beliefs with respectful, yielding and grateful communication and intention.

Propagation of this doctrine may occur through sharing its principles and witnessing the examples of one aiming to align with the principles of the House of Light and Chaos and aim to align with the one's true self. Respectful communication is encouraged; this may be exemplified by responding mindfully to inquiries, seeking permission before discussing or asking about one's or another's identity, which may include beliefs, practices, and rituals, all without imposing one's own judgment and or limiting one's criticism. Hakikintentio is encouraged, respecting oneself and others, being mindful when to yield and allowing gratitude to be constant and present within one's realm of interaction.

Additionally, sharing resources such as food, aid or guidance to wildlife and or those in need, as judged by their own perspective, embodies the principles of the House of Light and Chaos. This doctrine aims to increase awareness of the constant choices one has available to makes or not make. This awareness may foster a deeper understanding of one true self by reflecting on decisions made or actions taken, or not taken.

There is no requirement for ceremonial gatherings for praise, worship, or acknowledgment. A commitment to consistent and deliberate actions and decision in according to one's principles and resolve is encouraged.

'The Impetus Six' of the House of Light and Chaos:

Superbia | Conscientia | Humilitas
(Pride | Awareness | Humility)

Avaritia | Aequabilitas | Generositas
(Greed | Fairness | Generosity)

Ira | Compositio | Patientia
(Anger | Composure | Patience)

Invidia | Acceptatio | Contentamentum
(Envy | Acceptance | Contentment)

Luxuria | Moderatio | Castitas
(Lust | Moderation | Chastity)

Desidia | Temperantia | Diligentia
(Sloth | Temperance | Diligence)

The 'Six Keys of Reflection' of the House of Light and Chaos: Questions or answers pend the perspective. Where, what, when, who, why, and how—or the existential six. The six keys or questions of reflection may guide one to the answers one seeks. It is encouraged that one is mindful of both the questions and the answers one seeks.

It is encouraged to have little answers to those questions as many answers may only truly be accurate given circumstance. Within this doctrine, one has space to write many questions, these questions may allow one to become closer or more aligned when oneself, even if not answered. One is encouraged to share questions with others on the journey towards oneself.

It is an accepted perspective that all are on a journey towards oneself on a spectrum of mindful deliberation and unintentional ignorance.

Embracing Questions and Answers: The existential six – Who, What, When, Where, Why, and How – serve as guiding lights on one's journey. Questions, inquiries, wonders and ponders have many starters and one is encouraged to explore. One is encouraged to be mindful of both the questions and answers communicated or not communicated with others and to oneself.

Value of Open Questions: It is encouraged to house many questions and hold fewer definitive answers, as true understanding often is not simple and require context and/or circumstance. This approach may allow for flexibility and adaptability in one's understanding.

A perspective accepted by the House of Light and Chaos is that belief is the primary where knowledge is secondary however knowledge is quite a tool such as anchor for reason of action and or inaction.

Space for Reflection: One is provided with space to document questions, an exercise that may bring one closer to or more aligned with oneself, even if and encouraged for these questions to remain unanswered if possible. This practice of reflection is an encouraged may be beneficial for personal growth and self-discovery.

Community of Inquiry: Sharing questions with others on one's own journeys is encouraged. This exchange of inquiries may foster a sense of community and shared exploration, as one seeks to understand oneself and the chaos around one on this journey. Encouraged mindfulness of inquiry and sharing without judgment often yields the ripest fruit with plenty seeds.

The House of Light and Chaos nurtures a space of collective wisdom, support and communication. The practice of non-judgmental sharing may improve mindful respecting, yielding and gratuitous actions and inactions and cultivate a nurturing and insightful existence within oneself and the realm with others.

Who

What

When

Where

Why

How

Made in United States
Troutdale, OR
06/29/2024